NATU... MVPS

VALUABLE BACTERIA

Tricia Hoffman

Gareth Stevens
PUBLISHING

Please visit our website, www.garethstevens.com. For a free color catalog of all our high-quality books, call toll free 1-800-542-2595 or fax 1-877-542-2596

Cataloging-in-Publication Data
Names: Hoffman, Tricia.
Title: Valuable bacteria / Tricia Hoffman.
Description: Buffalo, NY : Gareth Stevens Publishing, 2027. | Series: Nature's MVP | Includes glossary and index.
Identifiers: ISBN 9781482479485 (pbk.) | ISBN 9781482479492 (library bound) | ISBN 9781482479508 (ebook)
Subjects: LCSH: Bacteria--Juvenile literature.
Classification: LCC QR74.8 H644 2027 | DDC 579.3--dc23

Portions of this work were originally authored by Katie Kawa and published as *Creatures We Can't Live Without: We Need Bacteria*. All new material in this edition is authored by Tricia Hoffman.

Published in 2027 by
Gareth Stevens Publishing
2544 Clinton Street
Buffalo, NY 14224

Designer: Beeline Media and Design, Inc.
Editor: Tricia Hoffman

Photo credits: Cover, pp. 1 Lotus_studio/Shutterstock; cover and throughout interior (dot pattern) HITO STOUNTIO/Shutterstock.com; p. 3 ImageFlow/Shutterstock.com; p. 4 crystal light/Shutterstock.com; p. 5 Pixel-Shot/Shutterstock.com; p. 6 Hans Wismeijer/Shutterstock.com; p. 7 New Africa/Shutterstock.com; p. 8 Shawn Hempel/Shutterstock.com; p. 9 Kateryna Kon/Shutterstock.com; p. 10 vchal/Shutterstock.com; p. 11 Sinhyu Photographer/Shutterstock.com; p. 12 Proonty/Shutterstock.com; p. 13 Jamil Yasin/Shutterstock.com; p. 14 Tatiana Shepeleva/Shutterstock.com; p. 15 Corona Borealis Studio/Shutterstock.com; p. 16 Christos Georghiou/Shutterstock.com; p. 17 Inna Dodor/Shutterstock.com; p. 18 Billion Photos/Shutterstock.com; p. 20 PeopleImages/Shutterstock.com

Printed in China

CPSIA compliance information: Batch #QS27GS: For further information contact Gareth Stevens, New York, New York at 1-800-542-2595.

Contents

Bacteria Are Everywhere

Bacteria are all around us. They live everywhere—from water and soil to the inside of our bodies. Some of these bacteria are bad and can cause sickness. But many kinds of bacteria are actually helpful! We need them to keep our bodies healthy.

Bacteria are tiny **organisms** with only one **cell**. They come in different shapes. They're so small they can't be seen by human eyes. They can only be seen with a **microscope**. Organisms that are too small to be seen without a microscope, such as bacteria, are called microorganisms. These microorganisms are tiny but very important!

Valuable Info

Trillions of tiny bacteria live in your **intestines**. They help absorb **nutrients** and break down food.

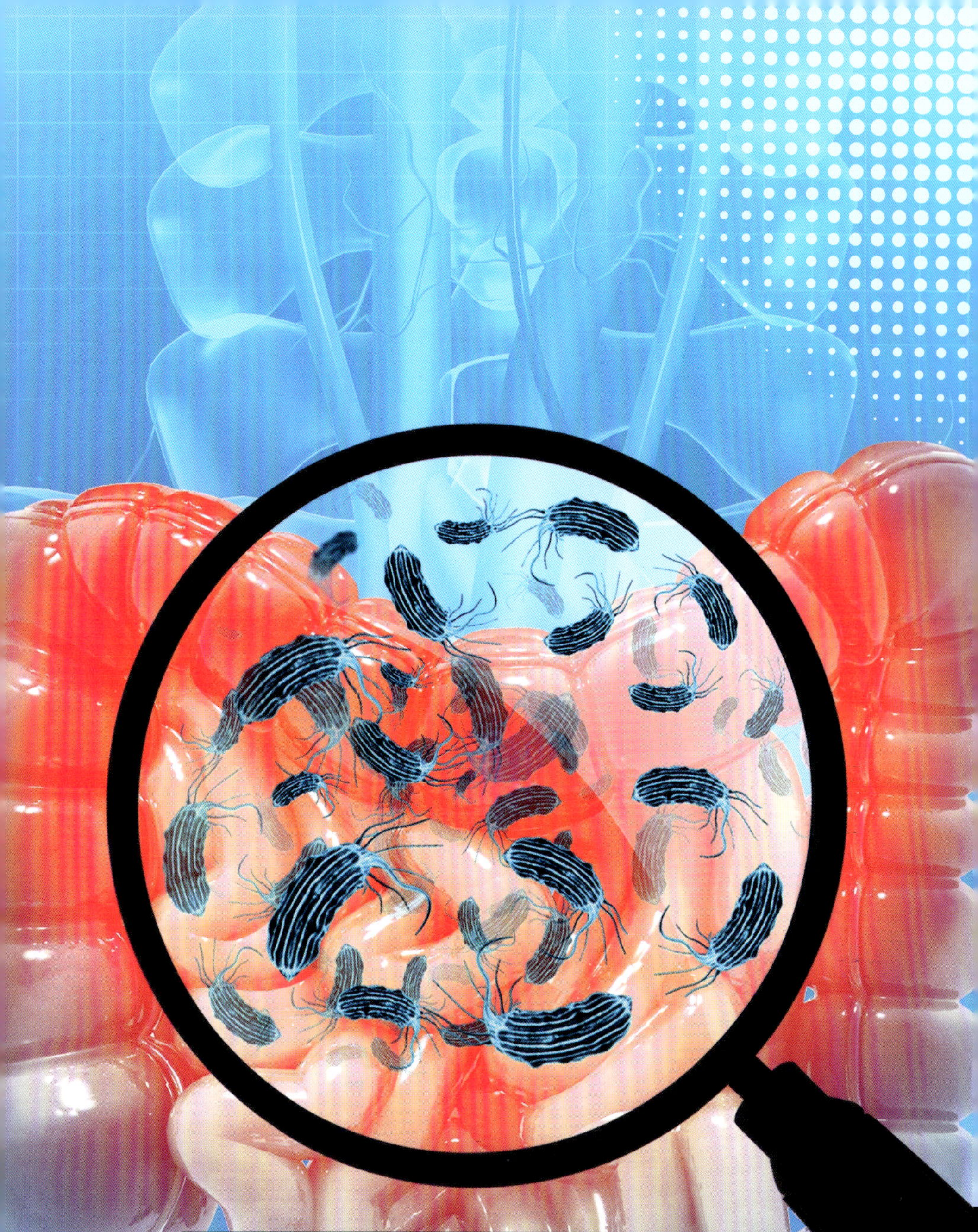

Many people think bacteria do nothing but spread sickness. But really, most bacteria are harmless. Some are even helpful!

Old Organisms

Scientists believe bacteria first appeared on Earth nearly 3.5 billion years ago. They can tell this by looking at **fossils** of bacteria, some of which are considered among the world's oldest fossils.

Because bacteria have been living on Earth for so long, they've **adapted** to life in almost every kind of habitat, or place where organisms can live. Some species, or kinds, of bacteria live in ice. Others live in water that's close to boiling. Some species of bacteria even live in clouds!

Valuable Info

Microorganisms such as bacteria are the oldest forms of life on Earth.

There are millions of bacteria in one spoonful of healthy soil.

The Cell of a Bacterium

Bacteria have only one cell. Each of these is called a bacterium. These cells look much different than those you would find in a plant or animal.

Plant and animal cells have a part called the nucleus, which is like the brain of the cell. It holds the cell's DNA, which controls what the cell does. A bacterium doesn't have a nucleus in its cell. Instead, DNA is spread throughout the cell. The DNA still controls the cell, though. Bacteria also have a cell wall. The cell wall gives a bacterium one of three shapes.

Valuable Info

Some bacteria move with the help of body parts that look like tails. They're called flagella. A single tail is called a flagellum.

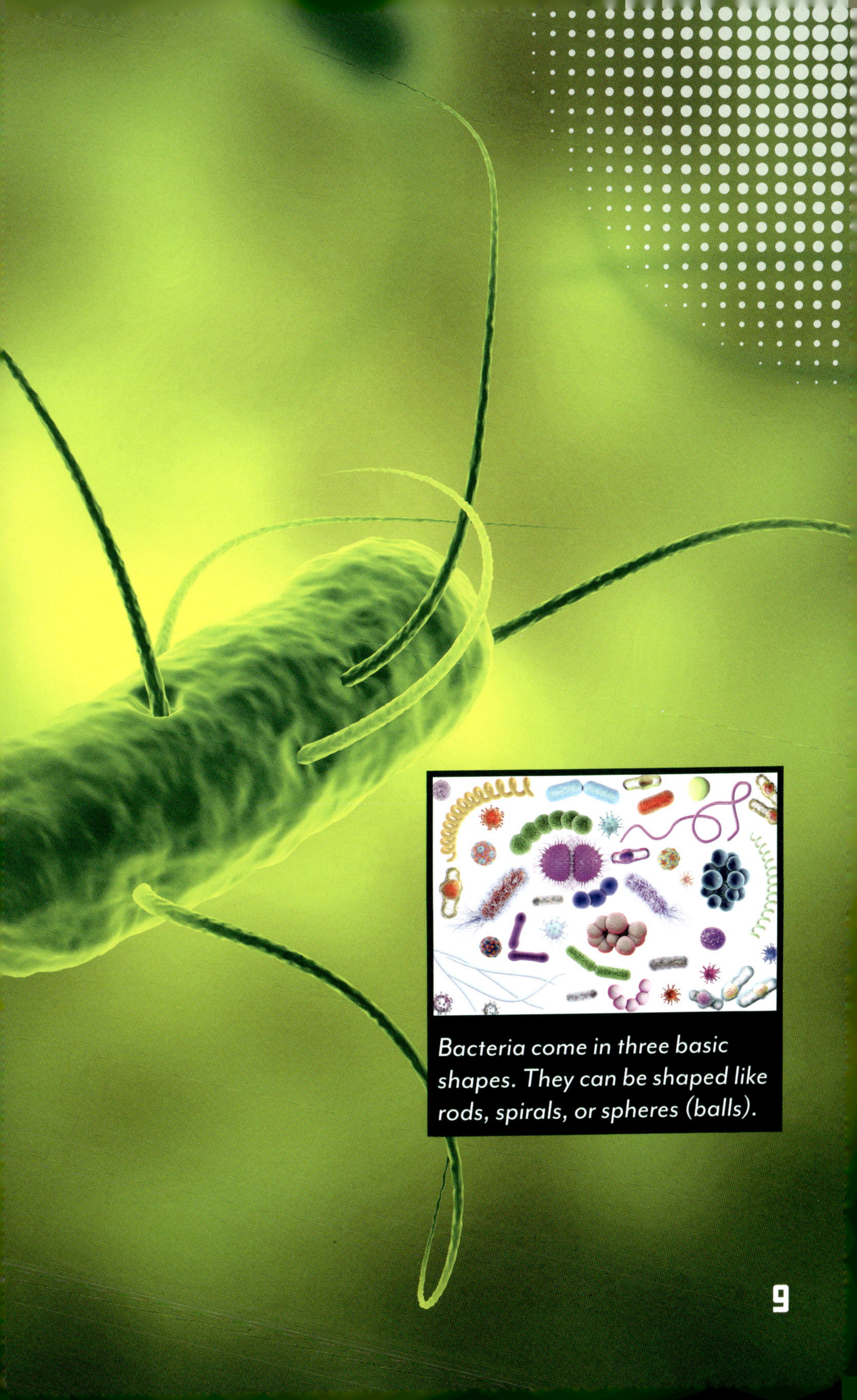

Bacteria come in three basic shapes. They can be shaped like rods, spirals, or spheres (balls).

More and More Bacteria

Bacteria reproduce, or make new bacteria, in different ways. Some grow new bacteria inside a mother cell. Others reproduce by budding. Budding happens when a growth, or bud, from one organism breaks away and becomes its own organism.

Most bacteria reproduce using a **process** called binary fission. For a cell to reproduce this way, it must first grow to twice its size. It must also make a copy of its DNA. Then, it breaks in two. This makes a new cell with the same DNA.

Valuable Info

Most bacteria can reproduce quickly. That's why people often worry about harmful bacteria spreading.

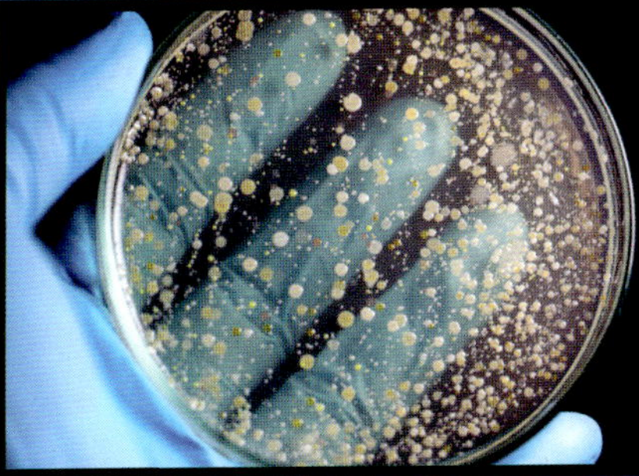

A group of bacteria that come from the same original cell is called a colony. A bacterial colony may look like just a dot on a **petri dish**.

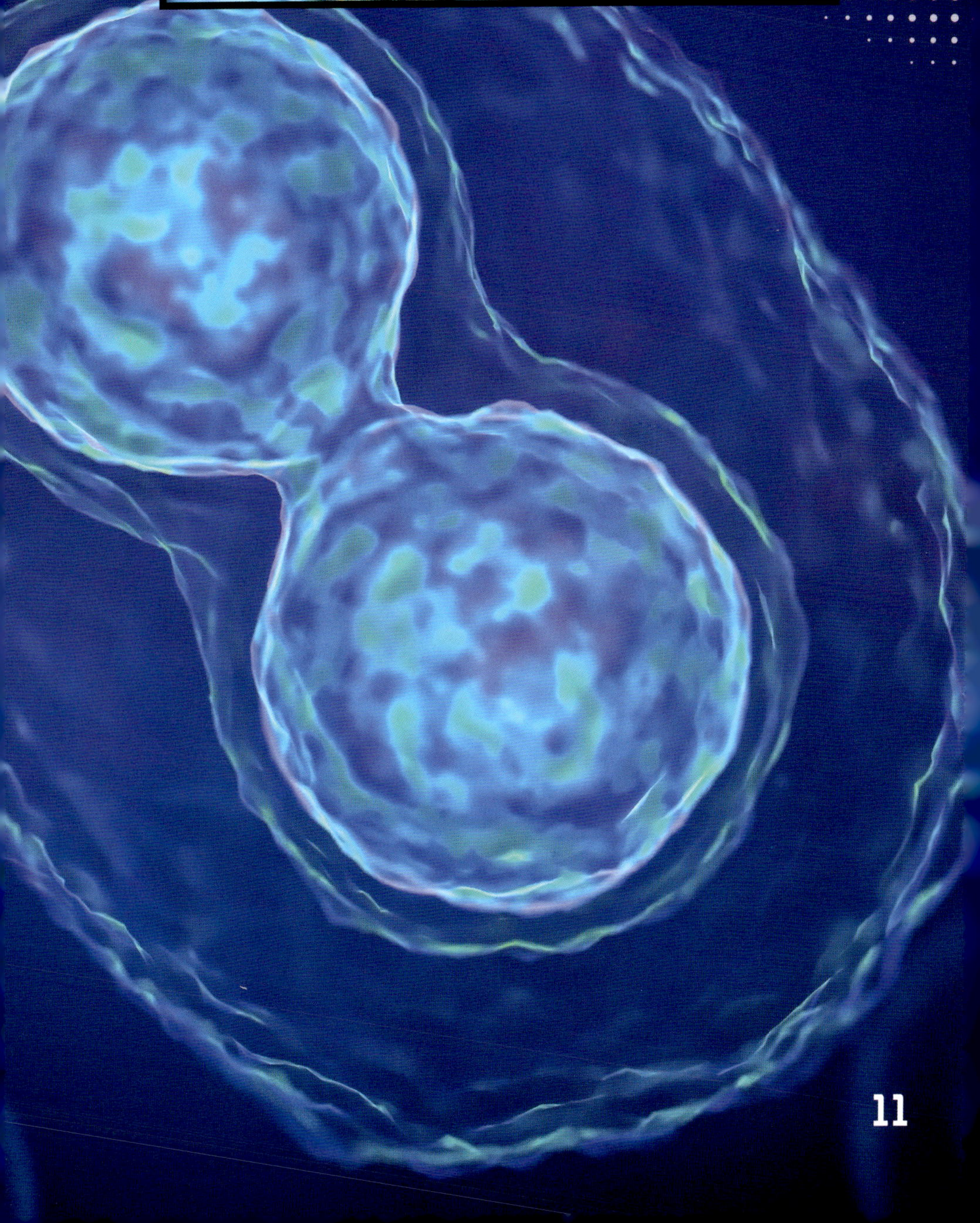

Bacteria in the Soil

Bacteria are everywhere around the world. They play a part in all ecosystems, or communities of living things. One place where they're especially helpful is in the soil. Without them, the soil wouldn't have the nutrients plants need to grow in it.

Bacteria in soil are decomposers. Decomposers are organisms that break down dead plants and animals. As they do this, they put nutrients back into the soil. Plants take in these nutrients through their roots. They use them to grow.

Valuable Info

Trillions of bacteria live in soil. The smell of fresh soil comes from the bacteria that live in it.

We need bacteria in the soil because we need healthy plants! Plants give us food and oxygen that we need to live.

Bacteria in Our Bodies

Bacteria are important in our bodies. They are a valuable part of our digestive system, which is the group of **organs** that breaks down the food we eat. The digestive system is also called the gut, and bacteria living here are sometimes called gut bacteria.

While harmful bacteria in your digestive system might give you a stomachache, most bacteria that live in this part of the body are there to help you. Bacteria in the digestive system work to help the body break down food and get the nutrients it needs. These helpful bacteria also work to **protect** against harmful bacteria that might make you sick.

Common bacteria found in the human digestive system are *E. coli*. You might have heard of *E. coli* because some kinds cause sickness. But many kinds actually help you!

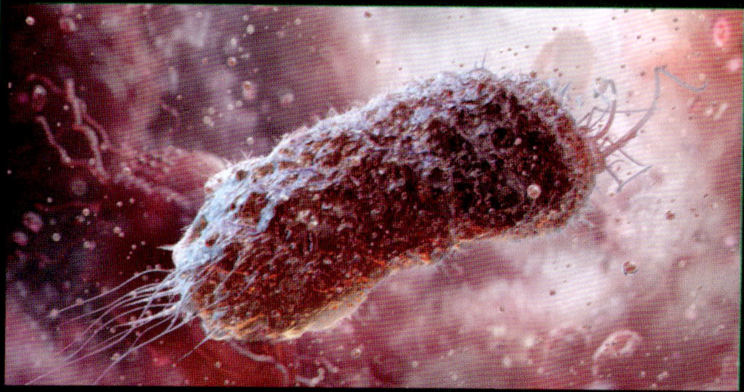

Valuable Info

Helpful bacteria in the digestive system can come from the foods we eat. They are sometimes called probiotics. Yogurt is often full of them!

An Immunity Boost

Bacteria are also an important part of the body's immune system. The immune system protects the body against organisms that don't belong there, including those that cause sickness. It is made up of special cells whose only job is to protect the body.

Scientists have found that having certain bacteria in the body helps immune cells grow and multiply. Without bacteria, our immune system would be much weaker. We would get sick more often. Bacteria boost our immune systems and help us stay healthy!

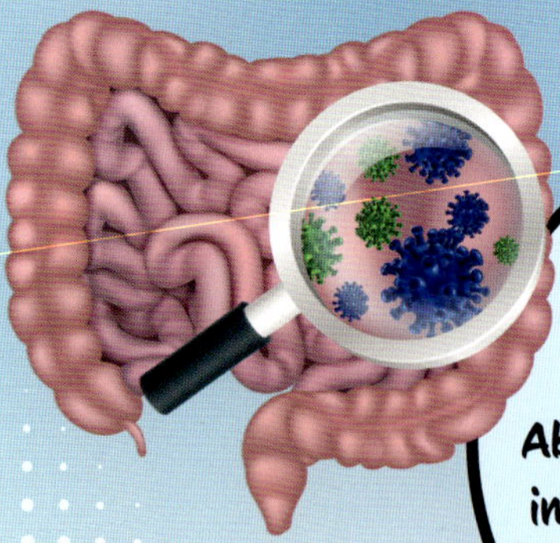

Valuable Info

About 70 percent of your immune cells are found in your digestive system.

Vaccines also help the immune system. A bacterial vaccine is a weakened or harmless form of a sickness-causing bacterium that's put into a person's body. Their body then learns to protect itself against it and keeps them from getting sick later on.

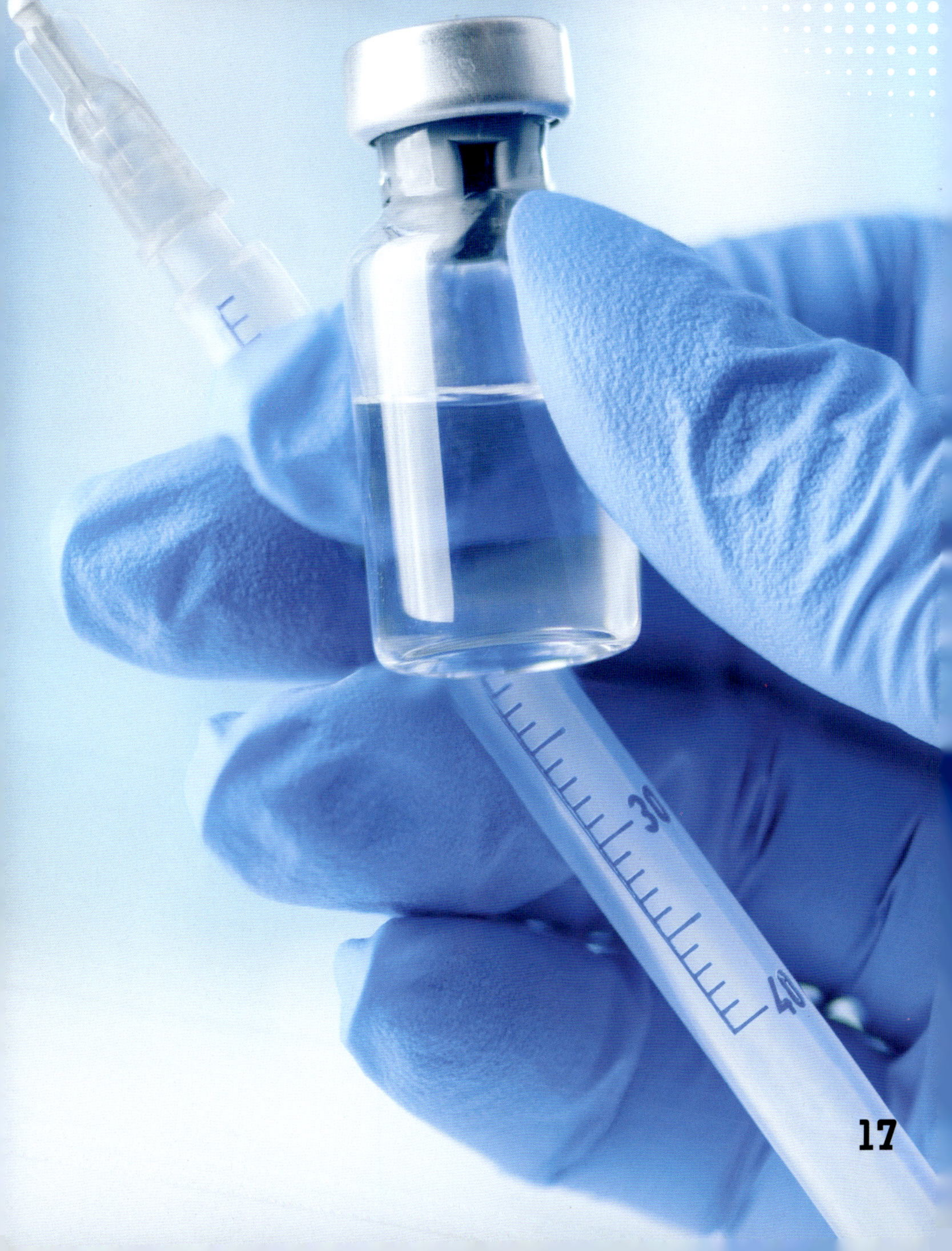

Harmful Bacteria

Sometimes people can get bacterial **infections**. These harmful bacteria can make people very sick. We call them "germs."

People try to get rid of harmful bacteria in different ways. Antibacterial soaps are used to kill bacteria on our skin. Antibiotics are medicines that kill bacteria in our body. Both help people get rid of harmful bacteria. However, taking too many antibiotics can also kill helpful bacteria in the digestive system, which makes it harder for the body to stay healthy. Antibiotics can only be prescribed by a doctor who knows when they are truly needed.

Valuable Info

Some harmful bacteria have become resistant to antibiotics. This means that medicines are no longer able to kill them.

Antibacterial soaps and antibiotics don't know which bacteria are helpful and which are harmful. They can kill good bacteria in our bodies too.

We Can't Live Without Them!

Bacteria are everywhere—and that's a good thing. They help plants grow in nutrient-rich soil so they can give us the food and oxygen we need. They help break down the food we eat and help our bodies absorb nutrients. And they help our immune cells grow and reproduce to keep us from getting sick.

Sometimes people need to kill harmful bacteria. To keep their bodies from losing too many good bacteria, they can eat foods like yogurt that put good bacteria back in. Good bacteria need to be protected. We can't live without them!

Valuable Info

Did you know that bacteria are used to make some of the foods we eat? They are used to make cheese, pickles, olives, bread, and more!

Scientists are always learning more about harmful and helpful kinds of bacteria.

Glossary

adapt: To change to fit new conditions.

cell: The smallest basic part of a living thing.

fossil: The hardened remains or trace of a living thing from a long time ago.

infection: A sickness caused by germs.

intestine: A long, winding tube in the human body that is made up of the small intestine and the large intestine. It helps the body take in nutrients from food and prepares waste to leave the body.

microscope: An instrument that uses lenses to show very small objects up close.

nutrient: Something taken in by a plant or animal that helps it grow and stay healthy.

organ: A body part that does a certain task.

organism: A living thing.

petri dish: A small, shallow dish that is used in scientific experiments.

process: A series of actions or changes.

protect: To keep safe.

Fact Check

1. Bacteria are tiny organisms with only one_____.
   a. leg
   b. cell
   c. nucleus
2. Bacteria come in three basic shapes: rods, spirals, or _____.
   a. cubes
   b. cylinders
   c. spheres
3. Bacteria living in our digestive systems are sometimes called______ bacteria.
   a. gut
   b. intestinal
   c. harmful

Answers: 1. b, 2. c, 3. a

On the Internet

Bacteria Facts for Kids
https://kids.kiddle.co/Bacteria
Learn about the different types of bacteria and the impact they have on our health and the environment.

Biology for Kids: Bacteria
www.ducksters.com/science/bacteria.php
What are bacteria? Read more about bacteria and where they're found. Then, take a quiz to test your knowledge!

Publisher's note to educators and parents: Our editors have carefully reviewed these websites to ensure that they are suitable for students. Many websites change frequently, however, and we cannot guarantee that a site's future contents will continue to meet our high standards of quality and educational value. Be advised that students should be closely supervised whenever they access the internet.

Index